DINNER WITH DEMONS

Jonathan Reynolds

BROADWAY PLAY PUBLISHING INC
New York
www.broadwayplaypublishing.com
info@broadwayplaypublishing.com

DINNER WITH DEMONS
© Copyright 2005 by Jonathan Reynolds

First printing: October 2005
I S B N: 0-88145-256-4

Book design: Marie Donovan
Word processing: Microsoft Word
Typographic controls: Xerox Ventura Publisher 2.0 P E
Typeface: Palatino

ALSO BY JONATHAN REYNOLDS

SIDEKICK
VITREOUS FLOATERS
STONEWALL JACKSON'S HOUSE
THE SCROTUM MONOLOGUES (one act)
LINES COMPOSED ABOVE TINTERN ABBEY,
  PART II (one act)
GENIUSES
STYNE AFTER STYNE (musical)
WHOOPEE! (musical, adapter)
TUNNEL FEVER OR THE SHEEP IS OUT
YANKS 3 DETROIT 0 TOP OF THE 7TH (one act)
RUBBERS (one act)
THE MARLBORO MAN (one act)
Escape (play for television)
Micki and Maude (screenplay)
Switching Channels (screenplay)
Leonard Part 6 (screenplay)
My Stepmother is an Alien (screenplay, co-author)
The Distinguished Gentleman (co-author)

DINNER WITH DEMONS was first produced by
Second Stage Theater, opening on 16 December 2003.
The cast and creative contributors were:

JOCKO . . . . Jonathan Reynolds

Director . . . . Peter Askin
Set design . . . . Heidi Ettinger
Lighting design . . . . .Kevin Adams
Sound design. . . . . .John Gromada

NOTES ON STAGE DIRECTIONS

The stage directions here are so detailed in order
to show how this complexly blocked and timed
production worked. They need not be followed
exactly and should be used only as a guide.

All cooking was done in front of the audience in
real time on a real stove and in a real oven with real
food—except for the deep-fried turkey. Because of New
York City fire laws, we were not allowed to maintain
an eight-gallon vat of boiling oil onstage. A clever
mechanism was rigged that looked like a turkey fryer
and that crackled and spattered when the real raw
turkey was lowered into it. At some point during
the play (I never knew when, which was just as well),
a stagehand crept under the floor and replaced the raw
turkey with a cooked one glistening with mineral oil.
When I lifted the "cooked" turkey from the mechanism,
more hisses, crackles, and dripping oil convinced the
audience this was a real event.

Further, food licensing restrictions forbade us
from feeding anyone in the audience, which was
unfortunate. The script begs for a little audience
interaction (apparently we could give away or re-
sell food made by someone else, just not by us).
By all means, if fire laws permit, deep fry the turkey
for real (though be aware it is extremely dangerous).
and if local laws allow, serve audience members bites
of food—if it's any good. Even without a deep fat fryer,
the stage was surrounded by fire extinguishers. A very

small fire did break out at one performance but was easily extinguished with a kitchen towel.

The timing of the cooking was arrived at backwards: knowing the potato soufflé had to emerge just before the Lee Remick story meant figuring out when it had to go into the oven so it would brown but not burn, and therefore when its preparation needed to begin. Same with the tomato sorbet and the cardoon. The apple pancake was a seat-of-the-pants work-in-progress every performance.

for Red
Salacious Muse, Eternal Squeeze

(Lights up on)

(A contemporary kitchen—which may contain un-contemporary fixtures: black Garland or red Aga range, Sub Zero fridge, all stainless or all-porcelain sinks, French blue cutting surfaces. Though a functioning kitchen in every respect, it doesn't look like something on The Food Network.)

(In the New York production, the work counter, sink, and four burners were D S C, the double ovens were U S L, and the turkey fryer S R. Against the back wall were foods in various stages of preparation, as noted, part of a table set for dinner [used in some scenes] was D S L, extending O S.)

(Before the curtain, someone has sautéed onions or duxelles or chicken stock, so that the smell perfumes the theatre by the time the house opens.)

(Lights pop on to discover JOCKO in front of counter holding a glass of wine)

JOCKO: *(Taking a deep breath)* Mmmm....I love that smell! Wouldn't it be great if everybody could afford to hire someone whose sole job it was to sneak in while you're sleeping and sauté up onions in butter? Chanel Number 6 as far as I'm concerned.
Get Elizabeth Taylor to come out of retirement and hawk it on T V.

(Husky Liz Taylor)

"White...onions."

Now let's see, better get back to my tomato sorbet... because I've got a bunch of people coming, and even giving them fifteen minutes for fashionable lateness,

they're going to be here pretty soon. Do you talk to
yourself in the kitchen? I do, all the time. I can't tell
if it's therapeutic or a scream for help.

(Paul McCartney's Let 'Em In *plays briefly and quietly in
the b.g.—just a hint of it.)*

*(He puts two tomatoes into boiling water, holds up a third,
very hard one.)*

Isn't it worse than what Saddam did to Iraq what's
become of our tomatoes? Hybred for durability so
they can be shipped from Nairobi to Mars in a
stagecoach without breaking, and they're tasteless
mush. These are of no use to anyone, except maybe
the Yankees for batting practice. Look at this.

*(He hits it with his fist, it doesn't break. He tosses it into the
trash, chops tomatoes)*

See ? And it's too bad, too, because in summer, when
the undoctored heirlooms come out, they're so sweet
and juicy you don't need anything with 'em except
maybe salt. Or a piece of bread and a little mayo.
I used to live in North Carolina, and when the German
Johnsons appeared in July, we'd just sit by the road and
eat 'em like apples, juices dribbling down our chins.
The first time I served this sorbet was in North
Carolina, and I didn't tell anyone at the table what it
was, and there were genuine, I think, "oohs" and
"ahhhs" until about halfway through somebody said,
"What is this?"
And I said, "Tomato sorbet," and there were a lot of
"Mmmms" and the conversation quickly turned to the
local election for sheriff.

(He empties boiling water into the sink.)

My mother never would've made this. Too exotic.
She was a WASP from New England, which means she
was sort of a WASP squared, and she thought anything

more elaborate than well done little lamb chops with
mint jelly was showing off.
You know how so many people who love food say
they learned to appreciate it because their mothers and
grandmothers were such wonderful cooks, and their
houses were always filled with the fragrance of a *pot au
feu* or a lamb *tagine* with preserved lemon?
Not me, boy. I was taught that mopping up the yolk
of a fried egg with a piece of white toast was *haute
cuisine*. And Mother wasn't very good at toast.

(Demonstrating)

See how fast you can get the skins off tomatoes? Boiling
water for ten-twenty seconds, they peel right off—and
they feel so good! Mmmmm, oozy and LEWD. Then
just chop them up.
Yes, Mother was an uninspired cook. Fortunately, when
the divorce came through and she came into all that
money, she gave it up. She hired what used to be called
a maid...who unfortunately proceeded to serve well
done little lamb chops with mint jelly every night.

*(Crossing to blender, attaching jar to blender, adding
ingredients)*

Now let's see...a little lemon juice, Worcestershire for
insouciance—

(Adding excessive Tabasco)

—a little Tabasco to keep everyone on his toes, a couple
of evil little anchovies...and some basil—or you can use
dill, but I'm sick of dill—salt but not too much because
of the 'chovies, black pepper, and a little grenadine to
lock in the color, then...technology!

(Pureeing the tomato mixture)

I'd wait till Mother and my sister Nancy were asleep,
and switch on Jack Paar, who used to be host of the

Tonight show and was very funny and sort of a rebel himself, then—

(Tasting mixture, adding more Tabasco)

—then about midnight I'd tiptoe into the kitchen and whip up very simple, two-step concoctions. For some reason I got very attached to grits for a couple of months—I don't know why, I was brought up in New York. Maybe it's because I was born in Arkansas, and a bunch of hominy snuck into my mother's breast milk at the hospital—

(He X U S C with blender contents to ice cream machine.)

—and I'd mix them with butter and then the next night grits with honey and nuts, then grits with maple syrup and for a few nights just food coloring...so I'd wind up with blue grits or green grits. Sometimes I'd get ambitious and heat up a can of chili and mix it with the grits. Gross, huh? But I've learned that one of life's great lessons is never argue with anybody's comfort food.
Whatever gets you through childhood and adolescence—whether it's blue grits and chili or salsa on ice cream, it's as sacred as your copy of *Goodnight Moon*.

(He pours the puree into an ice cream maker, puts it out of the way so it can't be heard.)

Now we want to give the sorbet a whir in the ice cream machine, and in thirty minutes or so you'll have the perfect hot weather appetizer which is even better in December because even though all the best tomatoes are on vacation, it's so surprising. Just don't tell anybody what it is.

(He X to sink, washes out blender jar.)

Some nights I couldn't sleep and after Jack Paar went off the air I'd write short stories. Man, writing until dawn, huddled with contraband food, was such a cool, private crime.

(He X U R carrying blender and stashes it, then returns to sink to clean up.)

My midnight grits raids occurred during a fairly tortured adolescence. I was this sort of rich kid who didn't know he was a rich kid and so what's the point? My sister and I grew up on the Upper East Side—1035 Fifth Avenue, on 85th Street. When the divorce came through, Mother moved us into a duplex on 72nd Street complete with hundreds of brass-polishers and white-gloved doormen straight out of *The Last Laugh*, the silent film by F W Murnau, which I believe was the first and last movie ever made about a doorman.

(He X to sink, cleans up.)

In those days show biz wasn't very kind to mothers; they weren't treated like saints they way they are today. *The Glass Menagerie, Gypsy, Rebel Without a Cause* made them all monsters, responsible for everything from rumbles in the Bronx to the crippling disease called homosexuality. Of all the unfair human dynamics, the darkest and most arbitrary is that kids don't have nearly as much influence on their parents as their parents do on them. I mean parents seep right into their poor kids' bones at the moment of birth, if not before. But children have no influence whatever over the first twenty to forty years of their parents' lives. Of course, kids are around long enough to get revenge on their parents. Isn't it going to be fun to see what happens when little Lourdes Ciccone turns fifteen?

(He removes turkey from the fridge, X D L, puts it on the counter.)

You know how some people can leave home and never think about their parents again, and others have them rattling around in their heads for eighty or ninety

years? I'm one of those. Take tonight. I'm making
dinner here for people I love who are alive—my main
squeeze Red, my two sons Eddie and Frank, Red's
kids, North, Nash, and Dodge—what imaginative
lives they're going to have—my sister Nancy, my half-
brother Don, great friends Oliver, Rafe, Gary, the
Baums if they can make it in from L A, Bridget,
Morosini, and Carvalho. And who keeps popping up in
my head? My mother, my father, and my Uncle Bus.
Even though my mother died almost forty years ago,
and my father ten, and my Uncle Bus twenty, their
images keep popping up in my head all the time.
For instance, whenever I'm faced with physical
danger—hardly ever, I see to that—my mother appears
because she was such a cautious and frightened person
by the time I was born. "Be careful! Watch out! Don't
climb that tree! Stay away from those boys! Try not
to fall down now!" Her basic philosophy of life was,
"Whatever it is, don't do it." So I became a physical
coward. I fear heights, I fear depths, I basically fear sea
level. I have to be Valiummed before getting a flu shot.

(Injecting turkey)

This won't hurt a bit, son. I'm also terrified by
nature—though that's just common sense.

(Continuing to inject turkey)

And whenever anything to do with money or women
comes up, my father boings into my head because he
was such an insanely brilliant businessman and had a
Ph.D in *broads*. And when a question of ethics or taste
or decency arises, there's my Uncle Bus as if he were
alive right now. It never occurred to them, but in my
mind, there was a constant struggle between Dad and
Uncle Bus for who I was going to become like. How'd
it turn out, do you think?
Here I'm injecting the internal baste for the turkey. It'll
keep that satanic white meat from drying out, which is

the curse of all turkeys, as you know. It's just some
Chanel Number 6 and garlic and spices. You can also
put Mr. Tom in a salt brine overnight, but this is faster
and goes deeper. Oh, you can get the recipes for all
these dishes in the lobby at the usual Broadway
markup of eight thousand percent.

(He rubs the turkey breast under the skin.)

Did you know you could get *under* a turkey's skin?
It's easy—and mmmmm, feels so good! Even better
than those tomatoes.
They ought to send these off to prisons once a week,
it'd cut down on a lot of trouble.

(Rubbing in cayenne pepper)

This is cayenne pepper just to give it a little bite.
Mmmmm... Man, my Uncle Bus would have loved
this bird. He and his wife Margaret used to host family
Thanksgivings and Christmases in Boston, and we'd
all go up for it—sometimes twenty or thirty of us.
When he died, I tried to fill that role, which has been
one of the most rewarding things I've done. But he
never had a bird prepared like this. That boiling oil
you see Stage Right isn't to repel the hordes of
Visigoths who threaten this theatre from time to time,
but to deep fry this bird, which in my opinion is the
best way to cook it because the skin is crisper, the flesh
juicier, it's faster, and it has fewer calories. Whaaaat?
You'll see.
I'm not going to truss or tie this bird because the whole
point is to get the hot fat into all these wonderful
mysterious turkey crevices.

(Illustrating between thigh and breast suggestively)

Oh, it might look neater and like a schoolmarm if you
did, but what you want here is a hooker.

(He X S R with the turkey.)

What you don't want to do is deep fry a turkey indoors
because if the oil overflows into the flames, your house
might burn down and all your pets'll die. And we don't
want that, do we....

(He lowers the turkey into the oil. It bubbles excitingly.)

So we just slip this in...gets sort of nicely violent,
doesn't it...and strangely relaxing. Oh, the reason
it has fewer calories is because no fat is absorbed.
Turkeys is waterproof!

(Finding someone in the audience)

But since this is one of the scarier things to cook and
might explode at any moment, will you keep an eye
on it and let me know if anything goes wrong?

(Lifting a fire extinguisher) We've got eight of these here,
which is almost enough to put out Donald Trump's
hair—if only someone would please please set fire to
it. I wish I could offer each of you mouthsful of this
largesse, but I can't because the lawyers here have
warned me that if I did, your lawyers—whom you
haven't even met yet—will crawl out from their caves
under the Manhattan Bridge and convince you you
were poisoned by the Pope's nose or the tomato sorbet
made you break out in peanuts. So I can't serve you
anything, but I can't serve *me* anything either, because
I'm advised that if I do my lawyer will sue me because
I've poisoned *me*. I'll win, and he'll collect a third.

(He retrieves wine from the fridge, X C counter.)

My father and mother and Uncle Bus all had such
profound relationships with food—everybody does.
You do, I do. Dad ravished it; Uncle Bus delighted in it;
Mother denied it.
When I think about my own sons, I wonder what
my influence on them has been. You make a vow as a
parent not to pass on the mistakes your parents made to

your kids. And what happens? *A,* not only do you pass those mistakes on, though maybe a little watered down, but *B,* you add a bunch of your own. Here, let me show you.

(He finishes wine in glass and retrieves oil from U L shelf, X counter, and pours oil into wine glass till it's half full.)

Suppose your father passes on a hundred percent of his indifference to you...

(Filling glass with grenadine)

And your mother passes on a hundred percent of her depression...

(Holds up glass)

Well, you're a good parent, so you pass on only fifty percent of this to your kids....

(Half filling another wine glass with oil-and grenadine mixture)

Now that boy's got a fighting chance.

(Overflowing the glass with Worcestershire)

Till you add a hundred percent of your own narcissism. Attica, twenty-five to life.
My parents separated when I was about fifteen minutes old. I vowed not to make the same mistake, so I waited till my boys were about fifteen years old. I don't know if it made any difference—same acrimonious divorce, thank you, California Bar Association. Well, maybe we'll see if it did tonight.

(Retrieving cardoon from fridge, then stripping and chopping them.)

Which brings me naturally to the mysterious cardoon. Looks like celery on steroids, tastes like artichoke without quite the struggle. They're very popular in France and Italy and probably started life in Sicily. The

Greeks loved them. You have to strip off the fibrous
parts, and they'll discolor if you don't add them to
acidulated water. "Acidulated" is a ten dollar word for
lemon in water, and I happen to have plenty of it right
here.

(Splashing the water)

They're wonderful baked with a little cheese into a
gratin, but I'm going to do them simply, just braised
in a little stock and butter and maybe a few surprises
from my wardrobe closet. I owe the cardoon a lot.

(Draining the cardoon)

You learn so much about yourself cooking. And it's a
great way to avoid writing. I've had more writers say
to me, "So that's how *you* don't write. Cool."

(Puting cardoon in stock)

I think there are about six things that really define
who you are, though right now I can only think of four:
whom you choose to be close to and love, your work,
sex, of course, and how you perform it...and how you
deal with food. Do you treat it like fuel or do you live
for
the next mouthful? Do you use it as a weapon—against
your parents or your kids? Or politically and go on a
hunger strike? How do you touch it—do you wrestle
with it and devour it with your hands, or always use
the right fork? Do you eat the same things day after day
or lunge for whatever's new?

(Pouring a glass of wine)

Through food, I discovered I was a sensualist, which
I already sort of knew, and generous, which had never
occurred to me. I like making and giving people this
lifestuff. Serendipitously, I found that a man cooking
turned out to be seductive. Not sure why.

(He X D R, sits in chair.)

But every woman I've asked, married or un-, claims
that a man cooking specifically for her (not, say, in a
restaurant, for money) is aphrodisiacal.

(Moonglow and The Theme From Picnic *plays in the
background)*

The first time was quite by accident. I invited a woman
over for dinner—let's call her Mary Alice...because
that's her name...put on some Erroll Garner and Miles
Davis...and *Moonglow and The Theme From Picnic,* the
most romantic music from the most romantic love scene
ever filmed...and brought out the first course, which
I'd made beforehand—*Shrimp Rothschild,* which you
make by hollowing out loaves of bread, sautéeing them
in clarified butter, fill them with shrimp poached in
fish stock, reduce the stock to a syrup, pour it over the
shrimp, and top it off with Gruyere cheese and a truffle
slice, into the oven.
She took one bite. "Oh," she said and followed me back
to the kitchen to watch me make the second course—
Tournedos Rossini—small filets of beef topped with
foie gras, truffle slice, and a Madeira reduction. "Ah."
She began asking very detailed questions about what
I was doing and who I was.
If you're lucky, there's a moment on a date when the
woman's eyes forget the background and focus on you.
She might laugh at an idiosyncrasy, or you mesh on
some point—a dislike of skiers, the realization that,
despite Hollywood screenwriting rules, people
basically aren't sympathetic—something. That's what
happened with Mary Alice.
But what cinched it for me was a spectacular creation
called *Le Talleyrand,* which you make with canned
cherries of all things and lots of ground almonds and
sugar, then cover them with a meringue and in the
meringue you put half an empty eggshell...into the

oven...thirty minutes later it comes out beautifully
bronzed. You lower the lights, warm up a little kirsch,
ignite it, pour it into the eggshell...it looks like a small
volcano...and that's when things can get really moist.

*(The music swells and plays together with SFX or film of
roiling waves crashing against rocks or anything to suddenly
make the kitchen seductive.)*

That's what happened with Mary Alice. Her eyes
were limpid and beseeching, "You are the deepest
and most complex man I've ever known...and I love
your knowledge and your hands...but I made another
date tonight at ten." And off she went to spend the
night with another guy! All my work went to benefit
him!...and he never even called to thank me.
After that debacle, I devised a few guidelines to
make future evenings go more successfully, which
I altruistically pass on to you.

(He X behind counter.)

First, make at least one of the courses ambitious.
A perfectly cooked chicken breast may be academically
brilliant, but it isn't going to accomplish what you
want—unless your date is Alice Waters.
Second, make something exotic, like , oh, I don't
know...cardoon! It'll make you seem adventurous
and a man of the world.
Third, don't make everything heavy or neither one of
you is going to want to take your clothes off.
Fourth, make sure you have plenty of cayenne around.
Cayenne covers up every conceivable cooking mistake
there is.
Fifth, don't apologize for anything. If you do happen
to burn something, you may be pleasantly surprised to
find that she thinks you did it on purpose. Or you can
always say, "I caramelized it."
Sixth, try to pull off at least one theatrical cooking
flourish—throw things around in a wok or flip

something in a pan or pour something from a great
height, like mint tea in a Moroccan restaurant.

(He pours tea from a great height.)

Seventh, never consult a cookbook in public. It's way
not sexy to watch someone follow instructions from a
book. Memorize the recipes or write them on little cards
and paste them all around—the way Marlon Brando
did when shooting *Last Tango in Paris*.
Eighth, make sure the woman you're cooking for
doesn't have another date at ten o'clock.

*(Moonglow and The Theme From Picnic swells.
He picks up the cardoon, tosses it into the fridge,
then dances like William Holden and Kim Novak.)*

Picnic starred William Holden...and Kim Novak.
I should know—I saw it thirteen times at age thirteen,
once for every year of my life.

(As William Holden)

"Hi. You make me feel...patient."
I was so in love with Kim Novak, I would have sold
several internal organs to meet her.

*(He X U S to get dishes for scene in Maxim's, sets the table
D L, and sits.)*

I never thought I would, but I was a pretty romantic
and persistent kid. When I was eleven, Marilyn Monroe
came to town. I phoned the *Herald-Tribune* to find out
where she was staying, called the hotel, and not
knowing any better, left the message, "Could you
please come over and spend the night?" Needless to
say, I never heard back. But two years later when I was
thirteen, Kim came to town promoting a stinker called
The Eddy Duchin Story—how could it be any good, she
dies halfway through—I was a much more worldly lad.
I bought her enormous bouquets of flowers and had
them delivered to her hotel suite at the Sherry on three

consecutive days. That got her on the phone!
"So...you're the one who sent me all the flowers.
Tell me about yourself."
"I...oh...um...well...could you come over and spend
the night?" There was a pause while she realized I was
thirteen.
"I'm kind of busy, " she said.
But she didn't hang up. She was very nice. And when
Mother found out I'd charged the flowers to one of her
accounts, she hit the roof. There's this myth about New
England women being too chilly to ever get emotional
or shout.

(Miming a cigarette as Mother. Quietly:)

"You'll pay for those flowers if it takes eight years."
Sure sounded like shouting to me. I wish my sons could
have known their grandmother—not because she
would have been so wonderful to them, but so they'd
know how lucky they are with the mother they've got.
I was always locked in combat with mine. She had no
idea what to do with me. And her sense of punishment
was so out of proportion. One night we got into an
argument over which T V program to watch, and she
called in the cops. Uniformed policemen right in my
bedroom!

(He X U S R to get mashed potatoes.)

Ever since I can remember, when serious Mother
trouble showed up, I'd switch off and view it as though
it was happening to somebody else—and that it was
funny. I used to call Mother "The Warden," which
infuriated her but cracked up my friends. In twenty/ten
hindsight, I see I was very tough on her. I just didn't
know any better. It turned out she'd been a rebellious
kid, too—but by the time I arrived, life and men ihad
knocked the feistiness out of her and turned it inward.

(Separating eggs)

Now here I'm making a potato soufflé which is unusual because it takes extra egg yolks instead of egg whites, and so it won't rise like your typical chocolate souffle or cheese soufflé, but it will be richer, balancing the cardoon and tomato sorbet. Little cilantro, salt and peppy...

(He plops the yolks into the soufflé, mixes them with cilantro, salt, and pepper.)

She would never have had the courage to call the cops by herself that night...

(He X S L with soufflé, puts it down, retrieves knife from rack on side of the oven, and hones it.)

...but behind every great passive-aggressive is a great aggressive-aggressive egging her on...

(He X behind counter to chop garlic.)

...and hers was a lawyer named Fred, a courtly Virginian who'd made a killing for her in the divorce and was now on twenty-four-hour house call. Fred was married but childless, so he knew even less about raising children than she did. I hesitate to tell you his last name because it's so Dickensian you'll think I'm making it up. It was Schlater— *(Pronounced "slaughter")* —Fred Schlater, and what I'd really like to be cooking up tonight is grilled lawyer.

(Smashing garlic with knife)

WHACK WHACK, barrister fricasee!
When I was fourteen I fell in love with the picture of a girl in Miami Beach. I'd talked to her on the phone a couple of times, and I just loved her picture....

(He X U L to retrieve bread crumbs and soufflé dish.)

I stole mother's driver's license so I could forge it and fly down there, rent a car, and impress the hell out of her. I even had a little beard made so I'd look

twenty-five and could fool Hertz. Unfortunately,
I didn't know how to drive—let alone drive and
smoke at the same time. So while lighting a cigarette
and making a left off Collins Avenue—which I can't
even do *today*—I totalled the car. Ripped the entire side
right off that beautiful '57 Chevy.
Oh, here I'm buttering and bread crumbing this soufflé
dish. Why bread crumbs? They make the eggs cling to
the sides and help them rise.

*(He spreads potatoes, adds mozzarella, covers them with more
potatoes, brushes it with butter and bread crumbs.)*

The police came in a nanosecond, and started to take
me downtown for a mug shot and fingerprints, and I
said,

"Officer, officer, is there anything I can do to *not* go
downtown?"

"What have you got?"

And from a lifetime of movie-going I knew he meant
money.

"I've got two hundred dollars in traveler's checks."

"No travelers' checks."

"I've got ninety dollars in cash."

"That'll do."

He took the money...and they drove me to the girl's
house...and *that* impressed her.

(He X counter, chunks the cheese.)

Now I'm going to add chunks of Bra Tenero, a mild
Italian cheese—or you could make it a little sharper
with a blue or even a Liederkranz if you could ever
find it.
When I arrived back at Idlewild Airport—which J F K

was then called—waiting for me was The Warden and Fred.

(As Fred)

"Johnny, your mother has something to say to you. Miss Edith?"

(As Mother, smoking)

"You are one step away from reform school, bub."

...which segued into dinner with guess who and guess what—Fred sure put away an awful lot of those well done little lamb chops over the years.

(As Fred)

"Johnny, you are going to learn to obey your mother."

"What if she's wrong?"

(As Fred)

"As far as you are concerned, she is never wrong!"

(As Mother)

"At least I wouldn't have forged my mother's driver's license."

"Your mother didn't have a driver's license— she couldn't drive."

(As Fred)

"Johnny—!"

"All right, all right, I made a mistake. But I'm a kid—that's my job."

(As Mother)

"You are going to a new school. And if you fail there, it won't be just the reformatory, it will be the penitentiary."

"And then what—the guillotine?"

(As Mother)

"Eat your dinner!"

"But Mother, these lamb chops are gray. And they're hard."

(As Mother)

"Lamb must be cooked to a hundred and seventy degrees or you'll get trichynosis."

"That's pork—and it's not even true of pork."

(As Fred)

"Johnny, we are up to here with your stupid smart remarks!"

"Fred, how can a remark be stupid and smart at the same time?"

And so it went, night after night. Oh, I was a son-of-a-bitch all right. Just couldn't let the old folks get away with anything. I saw the world with the piercing light of honesty—ya know, like every teen-ager. I did pretty well at my new school, but The Warden and I continued our arguments on the phone. The night before one of the vacations, I told her I wanted to go out to dinner with my friend Harry Hoole.

"No."

"Why not?"

"It's your first night back."

"So?"

"You're always trying to get away with something."

"No I'm not, we just want to go out for burgers, food we don't get at school, we're not going to rob a bank."

"How do I know that?"

"How do you know I'm not going to rob a bank?"

"Yes. Prove it."

"How do I prove I'm not going to rob a bank?"

"By not going out to dinner with Harry Hoole your first night back."

"Well what's to stop me from robbing a bank my second night back?"

"I knew it!"

"Mother—"

"You've got to learn to obey me—"

"No I don't!"

"Yes you do!"

"Oh no I don't!"

Well, when the bus from school pulled into Port Authority the next day, there waiting for me was the Warden, Fred, and a man so huge his knuckles dragged on the concrete.

(As Fred)

"Johnny, your mother's got something to say to you. Miss Edith?"

(As Mother, smoking)

"This is ex-police Lieutenant Walker. You will be spending the week end at his house as punishment. Lieutenant Walker, there is to be no television and no dessert."

And off I was whisked to Queens to spend the week-end with ex-police lieutenant Walker. And there was no T V, and no dessert, but as punishment goes, it wasn't all that bad—he gave me driving lessons. When I got back to the city on Monday I was more determined than ever to see Harry—this was now war between the Warden and me. We came up with a

scheme and got a girl from school to impersonate her
mother on the phone and invite us all to dinner in
Pelham. The Warden bought it.

(He puts the soufflé in the oven.)

Four hundred degrees for thirty minutes. On the train
to Pelham, Harry and I came up with a plan to snow
the two girls we were really going to meet in the bar
in Pelham. Existentialism was all the rage then even
though nobody understood it, and *Being and
Nothingness* was the hot cult book even though
nobody had read it. I, however, had read the *Cliff Notes*.
So when we got to the bar, I immediately brought up
existentialism with the two girls, Pat and Sue.

"It's...a quasi-cyclical system notioning the rictus that
alienates us all in an irrational and unreliable world."

"No it isn't," said Pat.

"It's about man's inhumanity to man," said Sue.

Uh-oh. They'd read the book. Suddenly, Harry looked
up and said,

"My God, Reynolds, there's your mother."

And in walks The Warden, Fred, and ex-police
Lieutenant Walker.

(As Fred)

"There he is! Be careful, he's a slippery one! Cover those
doors!"

As if I were Charlie Starkweather. The bar went dead
silent. Fred and the Warden walked straight over to me.

(As Fred)

"Johnny, your mother has something to say to you.
Miss Edith?"

But before she could say anything, I stood up and turned to my friends.

"Messeiursdames, this is *Being and Nothingness,"*

and exited the bar with visions of women's underwear strewn in my wake.
I spent the next two days locked in my room trying to live down my humiliation which, despite the bravado, was total. This time it was only bread and water.
I'd spent twelve of sixteen vacation days incarcerated, though admittedly in fairly upper middle class incarceration.
I eventually realized Mother just wanted control over *something* in her life.
She certainly had no say with her overbearing father or her misbehaving husband, and now Nancy was ignoring her pleas to stay on the marriage track and left Brearley to join the New York City Ballet...which to Mother was worse than wearing stiletto heels and swinging a purse on 8th Avenue. So I became the lucky sparring partner.
She tried hard to find a man—oh, not for her, she never dated. For me. But ex-cops? Fred? I think The Warden and I would have stayed locked in combat for all eternity if it hadn't been for my Uncle Bus.

(The timer on the ice cream maker rings.)

Le sorbet est pret!

(He rushes up to the sorbet, wheels it behind the prep counter.)

His real name was Frank Remick. He was Mother's brother, father of actress Lee and aspiring rancher Bruce, stepfather of three girls, and the most elegant man ever to grace the boulevards of New York, Boston, and Quincy, Massachusetts.

(Removing a tray of four to six sorbet bowls from fridge)

Simultaneously masculine and refined, he introduced
me to prime beef *without* ketchup, jazz, red wine, and
the proper perspective—all humor—toward *North by
Northwest.*

(Scooping sorbet into bowls)

He looked like the love child of Cary Grant and William
Holden, spoke in a mellifluous baritone, and smoked
cigarettes beautifully, using a long holder.

(Referring to sorbet)

Isn't this color brilliant? You'd eat it if you didn't know
what it was, wouldn't you?
He reminded me of George Bailey in *It's a Wonderful
Life*. He dreamed of high finance in London and Paris
but when his father died suddenly of a heart attack
during Uncle Bus's senior year at Harvard, he gave
up his dreams and took over the family department
store, Remick's of Quincy, so his mother and two sisters
wouldn't be left floundering and possibly broke. He
wound up loving the retail business and made an
enormous success of it, and after a few years bought
it from the women at a considerable profit to them.
But a few years later, The Warden decided the price
wasn't fair and, badgered by Fred Schlater, sued him.
How does *poached* attorney sound? The judge
eventually threw the case out for being frivolous,
but law suits take a long time, and in that period Bus
had his first heart attack. So he wasn't all that kindly
disposed toward the Reynolds side of the family.

(He puts the sorbet tray into the freezer.)

But when I was thrown out of my eighty-third school,
Mother phoned him for help. Dad was completely out
of the picture, building his empire out west.
By rights, Uncle Bus should have had nothing to do
with his litigious sister or her trouble-making son. But

one night he flew down to New York and took me to
dinner at a very swank hotel.

(Lights dim, restaurant sounds are heard, and JOCKO *sits
behind the prep counter re-enacting dinner.)*

I remember the menu was huge and covered with
calligraphy.
I was pretty suspicious. Was I going to get another
"Your mother's had a hard life, be a good boy" lecture?

"What would you like to order?"

"What's pheasant under glass?" I'd vaguely heard
about it in a play as the ritziest thing you could eat.

"It's a little like chicken, but gamier," he said.
"Why don't you try it?"

"So expensive!"

"That's why I had them put it on the menu."

We laughed, and I ordered it. I was still pretty
suspicious. He found out I was an expert on Elvis
and jumped right in.

"That boy is so *alive*," he said, unlike any other person
his age. "And the songs he chooses are so
witty"—*witty?*—
"*Hound Dog, Blue Suede Shoes.* And that *Heartbreak Hotel*
is practically Greek tragedy." I'd never heard that
before. He was genuinely interested, not talking down.
"Do you like the Red Sox?"

"I did before they became the Yankee farm team."

"Low blow. Well, this year we're going to get
our freedom back. When you come up to Boston,
I'll take you to Fenway. The store has a box."

"I'll skip school tomorrow!"

"No, tomorrow night I'm seeing your sister dance."
Why was he doing this? "Do you like the ballet?"

"It's okay...but you'd think with all that beauty they could keep the toe shoes from making such a racket."

"Silent toeshoes? I like it. Let's market them. Why don't you tell Mister Balanchine? That's her boss."

Elvis, baseball *and* the ballet? Was this a trick? He slipped a cigarette into its holder.

(He reveals a pheasant under glass, as described.)

The pheasant arrived but didn't look nearly as glamorous as I'd hoped. I'd expected a huge platter, with bright plumage, maybe trumpets in the background. Instead, there were two small beige poultry breasts covered with what I called gravy and he called sauce, and the "under glass" part just looked like fog. The waiter lifted the dome, and I backed away to avoid the steam. But Uncle Bus waved the vapors toward his nose.
"That's the point, you see. The glass concentrates the aroma, so you can smell it. Beautiful, isn't it?"
A Roman candle went off in my head. Smelling was part of eating?
Food could be beautiful? How rich life was outside my house!
The taste was bitter and chewy and had something nasty in it called Cognac, but I ate every bite, imitating everything he did—how he used his fork, the way he paused, how he crossed his legs. Because with that one gesture, that allowance— "You can have it"—he rescued me, the first of many times, from the dark.

(He pushes back from the counter. Count Basie plays, increasing in volume as indicated, and Joe Williams belts "All Right, Okay, You Win, I'm in Love With You," and he bops to the music.)

And when I'd visit him in Boston, he'd put on some platters late at night, and teach me how to listen to music—in the dark and LOUD. And when he'd come to

New York, he'd take me to Birdland where in sheer
volume (let alone transcendence), The Count Basie
Band with Joe Williams would have blown away
Nine Inch Nails.

*(Lights put him in silhouette as music blasts, and he X fridge,
removes sausage and swings it wildly in time to the music,
chops it, tosses it into the cardoon with abandon. When the
music stops, lights come up full and—)*

Nancy wasn't the only Reynolds to inherit the balletic
gene. Actually, she was. This is a little andouille to give
the cardoon some heft.
Dad dealt with food and me differently. Cut to eight
or nine years later. I'm in grad school in London,
on spring break with my girlfriend Anna in Paris—
first time there. Anna was very beautiful, with that
wonderfully intimidating English accent that's given
countless American men massive erections for the last
four hundred years.
Suddenly, Dad's on the phone. "Hi! I'm in town.
Where'd you like to have dinner?" I snapped to
attention.
I'd spent a few days with him the summer before at
his thirteen-acre lakefront property on the Nevada side
of Tahoe. His bedroom had *two* king-sized beds in it
right next to each other—looked like a football field.
I never knew if that was so he could fit more women in
there with him or sleep farther away from the one who
was there. He tried marriage—four times—in pursuit
of respectability, but couldn't make a go of any of them.
I was twenty-two, and it was the first time I'd ever
spent the night under the same roof with him.
Dad lived in—let's see—Arkansas, Oklahoma, Nevada,
California, Hawaii, and the Trump Tower in New York.
Not serially—all at the same time. He started hawking
newspapers as a boy and years later bought a lot of
them up. His usual M O was to take a small, failing,

family newspaper, fire the family, and turn them
profitable. Very profitable. At one point, he owned
about sixty of them. He was the first kid on the block to
own his own 727—which true to form he outfitted with
a king-size bed. He'd come back from the war restless
and constantly hit the road to find more newspapers
and, probably, dames. Mother finally got fed up, found
Fred Schlater, and together they sued him for one
million 1947 dollars. It was a very bitter divorce, which
gave Dad the excuse to ignore us ever after.
"What about dinner?" he growled into the Paris phone,
and since *Gigi* was the sum of my French restaurant
knowledge, I blurted out, "Maxim's," expecting him
to laugh. With the Warden still downstage center in my
brain, I assumed Maxim's and pleasure in general were
for others. But Dad and Uncle Bus had a different
take—those things were for *us*. Life was supposed to be
thrilling, a concept Mother never quite got.

*(Retrieving ice bucket, throwing ice into it, then a bottle of
champagne)*

"Maxim's, see you at nine," he said. It was always
electric when Dad came to town—and scary.

(He X D L, places champagne bucket on table.)

So Anna and I got as gussied up as grad students could
and swanned into Maxim's and *la belle époque*.
I ordered duck *à l'orange*, because it was the only thing
I'd heard of outside of *crepes suzettes*, which I also
ordered, not realizing that both were sweetened with
orange juice. Everything had sauce on it, all inspissated
with butters, flours, *crème fraiches*. It was delicious but a
little oppressive. *Nouvelle cuisine* was a decade away.

(As Anna)

"Were you here during the war, Mister Reynolds?"

(As Dad)

"Here, London, Australia, all over."

(As Anna)

"You sound as though you rather enjoyed it." Anna's family had lived through the blitz.

(As Dad)

"It was a hell of a war...but better than no war at all!"

Anna was aghast, which pleased him no end.
I told him how much I'd like to have a house like his in Tahoe some day.

"Do you *really* want to make money?" he asked.

"Well, yeah!" I said.

(As Dad)

"Oh, sure, everybody'd like to take a pill and be rich, but do you really want to do what it takes?"

"Yes!" But what was that exactly? What was the secret?

(As Dad)

"No secret. Big idea, start small, one foot in front of the other. Start by borrowing money from a bank."

"Why would a bank loan you money?"

(As Dad)

"Loan me money because I'm a good operator."

"What's a good operator?" Dad looked at me from miles away. This was going to be work, he could tell....
He might as well have been speaking Turkish. Anna, who was a socialist, asked him about his labor contracts.

(As Dad)

"What labor contracts? Don't have any labor contracts. Don't have any unions."

(As Anna)

"How ever did you manage that?"

(As Dad)

"A few years ago at my Las Vegas operation, deliverers went on strike. So I took out a truck and delivered the papers all day myself. When I came back to the plant, one of the strikers starts waving a picket sign in front of my windshield. Next thing I know, he throws himself down in the driveway."

(As Anna)

"What on earth did you do?"

(As Dad)

"Drove right over him. Broke his back. But I broke the strike, too! Only have to do something like that once, dear, word gets around." So that's what it took.

(As Anna)

"Well, well, didn't the police arrest you or anything?"

(As Dad)

"No! Why should they? It's my driveway. Don't expect somebody to be lying down in your own driveway, do you?"

I tried to talk about grad school, but Dad just couldn't see why anybody needed to go there.

"Graduate school's just another word for welfare!"

He couldn't enter my world, and I couldn't enter his. I got up and went to the loo and returned a few minutes later to find Anna wide-eyed. Dad was antsy and wanted to leave—

(Xing D S C)

—so we all went outside and looked up at the cloudless sky. It was beautiful. Suddenly, a shooting star went by, and he wished on it.

(As Dad)

"Moneymoneymoneymoney."

We thanked him profusely, and he hurried off to the Elysee Palace or wherever he was staying, and Anna and I descended into the Metro.

"Are all you Yanks like that?"

"I wish."

"Didja know your dad invited me back to Las Vegas with him?"

I was stunned. But...I wasn't really angry. I was sort of flattered. I'd finally done something he approved of so strongly that he wanted it for himself. My girlfriend!

"What did you say?"

"I said, 'I don't think that would be proper, Mister Reynolds, I'm in love with your son.' That stopped him, and he behaved like a perfect gentleman."

Stopped me, too, since Anna hadn't told *me* she was in love. Paris had suddenly become surprisingly romantic for all three of us.

(He X U L to turn on a burner.)

It's hard to find duck *à l'orange* in Paris anymore, and I don't plan to take my sons to Maxim's any time soon, with or without their girlfriends—just in case this sort of thing is genetic. On the other hand, maybe I will, because I realize in some areas at least, I behave a whole lot better than my Dad did.

(He X U L, gets spatula, sauté pan, and sugar, X stove.)

But every time I've been back, images of my old man making a move on my girl friend and driving over that poor picketer's back refresh themselves in my memory. And despite his ill-placed lechery and ruthlessness, I picture him adventurous, optimistic, unbridled, mean

as hell, sword drawn, mindless of his appearance and
what rules he broke, zipping around Europe courtesy
of the I R S, and I think...that son-of-a bitch.
Could he do this and still not get a crown?
Tut, were it further off, he'd pluck it down!
He was the most amazing man I ever met—and the
most selfish. He never would have lifted a finger if
I'd gotten in real trouble or, say, been arrested and
had to spend the night in jail.

(He X U R fridge for pancake batter.)

It may not come as much of a surprise to you that I did
get arrested and spent the night in jail once.
I was travelling around California the summer of my
senior year in college with a friend named Weed, and
the Monterey County police arrested us for trespassing
on Kim Novak's property. Her breathy vulnerability
never let me out of its clutches. And before we
knew it, Weed and I were being photographed and
fingerprinted in the Monterey County jail, and we spent
a sleepless night on cold concrete surrounded by the
local drunks and peeping toms. Bail was set at seven
hundred and fifty dollars apiece—or about ten large
by today's standards.
Both of us were terrified—not that the ferocious drunks
would sodomize us, but...what were we going to tell
our mommies and daddies? I knew if I called Dad, he'd
say, "You got yourself into this, you get yourself out."
And Mother! Would have phoned the sheriff: "Keep
him in there. Rent to follow."

(Melting butter in sauté pan)

Miraculously, Uncle Bus was vacationing with his wife
Margaret nearby, and he came right down and bailed
us out.

(As Uncle Bus)

"Did you at least get to see Kim?"

"No, she's in Europe."

(As Uncle Bus)

"Well, next time, better intelligence."

He was soooo cool about it. He and Margaret put
us back on the road with nary a word of criticism.
He knew how foolish I felt. I half expected him to slip
me a doggy bag with pheasant-under-glass in it, but by
then it was pretty much out of date, as would soon be
his blue blazer, rep tie, cigarette holder, and enormous
civility.

*(He sautes apple slices and pours batter over them when
appropriate.)*

Oh, here I'm preparing a Reubens' Apple Pancake,
which I learned from my buddy Ronnie, the grandson
of the original Reuben, Arnold, who also invented
the Reuben sandwich and about a hundred and forty
other sandwiches, all named after Sophie Tucker.
I'm sautéing these apples in butter, then pouring some
batter on top...evening it out...oh, this recipe uses all the
butter in Denmark and all the sugar in Cuba by the way.

(He sprinkles huge handsful of sugar on the Pancake.)

A little Cuba...a little more Cuba...
Uncle Bus died in 1983 after two or three more heart
attacks. I asked him after his penultimate one if there
was any pain.

"No. My left arm hurt a little, then I woke up in the
hospital."

He was smiling. It was a wonderful way to go—
for him. And murder on the rest of us. I never got
to tell him what he'd meant to me, and what a shining
example he was, and that in the battle over who I was
going to turn out like, he'd won.
A few years after Uncle Bus died, Dad came down with

dementia. His three business associates urged his
kids and grandkids to visit him in Hawaii as often as
possible. So twice a year, the four of us suited up and
off we went to Hawaii, my boys to live their childhood,
me still in search of mine.
It was simple to see why the associates wanted him
pre-occupied with family—so he wouldn't meddle in
what they increasingly considered to be *their* business.
Why, he might do anything—like get married, which
scared the hell out of them since if he had a widow,
she'd inherit their fortune.
In fact, he *did* propose marriage at least once more. But
either the son of-a-bitch himself or the sons-of-bitches
around him were so smart that he had previously
signed a piece of paper which said "If I ever say I want
to get married again, don't let me." They knew what
kind of trouble his raging libido could get him into. In
his dementia, he propositioned my wife, his daughter,
his granddaughter, a couple of masseuses, and the
keyhole of his bedroom. Here comes the tricky part...

*(He flips the pancake onto a cookie sheet, adds butter to the
pan.)*

A little Denmark..."Tricky" reminds me of the story the
very British director David Lean used to tell. Seems a
grizzled, penniless old man is seen in the company of
a singularly breathtaking young woman. "My God,"
says one observer, " what does she see in him?"
And the other says, "Tricky finish."

(He slides the pancake back into the pan.)

And while you're working on "tricky finish"...

(Sprinkling sugar)

...a little more Cuba...and a little *more* Cuba...I never
sang for my father, to quote my friend the playwright
Robert Anderson, but I did finally manage to cook for
him. Dad accepted an invitation to our modest house in

the mountains of North Carolina. Since he hated being in the same place longer than three days—even his own houses—I knew his stay wouldn't be long...just Armageddonian. At least I'd figured out what to cook. Whenever I'd visit him at his home in Hot Springs, Arkansas, he'd go to the racetrack where he had a thoroughbred horse with whom he felt increasing simpatico, and he'd order fried catfish. So I consulted a few cookbooks, found a catfish source, and mixed together some cornmeal and spices. Here comes the tricky part again.

(If the pancake is ready, he flips it onto the cookie sheet again, adds butter to the pan.)

A little Denmark...a little more Cuba. The day Dad and his 727 arrived in Winston-Salem with full entourage, we caravanned up the mountain, he had a nap, woke up in a fury , and threw a fit, shouting at everybody in our living room,
"Where's my money? Where's my money?"
I certainly didn't know—he sure hadn't given any of it to me. None of his handlers could calm him down.

"I don't know, Dad. In a bank in Little Rock? Or Tulsa? Or Kona?"

This was bewildering coming from a man whom *Forbes* magazine had recently dubbed a billionaire at a time when a billion dollars was a lot of money.

"How do you know! Have you seen it? Have you?"

"No, but your associates must have—"

"My associates? My associates are a bunch of crooks! My associates have been robbing me blind since 1897!"

Which would have been quite a feat, since that was nine years before he was born.
It took several minutes to talk him down from that window ledge, but the specter of winding up poor like

his father never left him.

I quickly threw together the fried catfish. He took several bites, mashed them in what remained of his teeth...and then his milky, alcohol drenched eyes which had overseen the creation of four thousand jobs and countless edifices where there had been none—softened, and for an instant there was connection, even appreciation. "You...did this...for me?" his eyes said...which was about the best that could be expected and all I'd been after all along.

(He puts the pancake in the oven.)

A few months later Dad died in his sleep. The 727 brought his body back to Las Vegas and he was cremated. And it seemed that before the ashes were soft his associates sold the company that was his life's blood and became very very *very* rich men. The bulk of his estate was left to a foundation, which like Nobel and Pulitzer before him, went to ease his entrance into the next life by assuaging his guilt for the crimes committed in this one. I probably will never forgive him for having such an exuberant, joyful, completely selfish life—and for never telling me what a good operator was.

(The turkey bell goes off.)

Turkey time!

(He heads for the turkey. The oven bell goes off, interrupting him.) Soufflé time!

(He runs to the oven, checks the soufflé.)

This can wait...and this can't.

(He runs back to the turkey, lifts it from the oil as McCartney's Let 'Em In *sneaks in.)*

Golden brown, just as threatened. Will you ever doubt me again?

(He puts the turkey on a platter, decorates it with greens and berries.)

Birds and meats need to rest a few minutes to let the juices retrench and the flavors develop. Aren't holidays something? Or aren't they? One of my last memories of The Warden, she threw me out of the house one Christmas because I'd grown a beard and was driving around in a third-hand hearse I'd bought. "The doormen are laughing at you behind your back and calling you Fidel!" It was the beginning of the sixties, and nobody had a beard except Castro and Allen Ginsberg, and no one at all had a hearse except Frank E Campbell..

(He X oven.)

So I spent Christmas day in Reubens Restaurant on 58th and 5th where Bergdorfs Mens' is now, feeling sorry for myself and eating this amazing amazing pancake, still the sweetest thing I've ever tasted, including *Le Talleyrand*. And it taught me one very important lesson: sometimes the best way to overcome self-pity is hedonism.

(He removes the soufflé from the oven, displays it to the audience.)

Yo yo yo, soufflé in the house!
Mother died when I was in grad school in London. She was sixty-two, smoked a lot, and had the Remick heart. At first I was jubilant—I was free from incessant combat, the tyranny of her censorship...then I felt completely abandoned. Argument and hostility can constitute a loving relationship, too, you know.
And then for years I had nightmares that she was hiding out in an apartment on the upper east side, just waiting for me.

(As Mother, smoking)

"I've been watching you...you've been bad...and I'm back!" Ooooof, cold sweats.

But then I realized she was the only person who mattered to me that I never cooked for. It never occurred to me to—I was an adolescent for so long... till yesterday, really.

(Drinking to her)

Well, I'm cooking for her tonight.
And then there was Lee.

(He sits D S R.)

I fell in love with her the way most people who met her did—at first sight, passionately, and like a sheepdog. I was maybe three, and she was probably nine, and we were on a beach somewhere, and had anything come of it, we both would have been in a whole lot of trouble in every state except Louisiana, because we were first cousins. Her life was golden, or that's how it looked from our side. We were the dysfunctional family, the Remicks were anointed. She seemed to clear every hurdle effortlessly, from her first Broadway play at sixteen to being chosen at twenty-one by Elia Kazan to appear in *A Face in the Crowd*.

She also married at twenty-one, a dashing T V director with a great future named Bill, and even after her marriage and well on her way to stardom, she'd phone up and say, "Jon—" she was the only one I never minded calling me that name, I always thought it so boring, Jon, "Jon, let's go see *Long Day's Journey Into Night*..." And off we'd go, she and Bill and I, four hours, changed the way I looked at everything. Theatre—and not incidentally, life—wasn't all *Pajama Game*. "Jon, let's go see *Sweet Smell of Success*—it was only a tough, savvy, hilarious movie then, and we began quoting from it right away: "I'd hate to take a bite out of you, Sidney, you're a cookie full of arsenic." "Cat's in the bag, bag's in the river, J J." We'd eat Italian and laugh

all the time. I was fourteen and felt very grown-up.
They had two beautiful children, she got nominated
for an Oscar, and became the midnight fantasy for
thousands of adolescent men and boys.
A few years later, I was thinking of getting married
but was mystified by the process and the repercussions,
as I am about most things. So at lunch one day, I asked
her, "Do you think I'm going to marry this woman?"

"Yes...I think you will."

"Do you think I should? I mean, you're taken, right?"

Fortunately, she laughed.

"Yes, I think you'd better!" she said.

So I did. And our family spent as many Thanksgivings
and Christmases with Lee and her second husband Kip
and their children at their house on Cape Cod as we
could, and together we'd cook up a storm. She loved
the kitchen and used to go to sleep at night reading
cookbooks. Life wasn't just good then, it was glorious.
And then in the spring of 1990 while she was filming a
T V movie, she said, "I've had this temperature about
one degree above normal for a few days.

"How many days?"

"Well, about a month."

When the film wrapped, she was told the cancer had
metastasized from her kidney to her lungs. She was
more astonished than upset.

"Isn't this curious—this happening to me." Denial is
murder in a relationship but sometimes can be one of
the more useful weapons in our psychological arsenal,
and Lee's refusal to clearly see or believe her fate wasn't
foolish—it was thrilling. What was also thrilling was
the reaction of her friends. Gangs of us gathered nightly
at her home to feed her, body and soul—and ours.

(Xing U S C behind counter)

One night I was making Chinese—six or seven dishes, and Lee was in the living room playing host to a dozen or so guests. She ambled slowly into the kitchen where I was. She used a cane now, eyes sleepy, swollen with steroids.

"What's all this?" she said.

"Sesame chicken, hotter than hell, made with a treeful of chilies and lots and lots of peanut butter, can you believe it?"

"Mmmm...I love Chinese," she said.

"One of the three great cuisines of the world."

"What are the others?"

"The three great cuisines of the world are French, Chinese, and Junk."

She took a little bite.

"Mmmm. Sooooo good."

"Can you taste things?"

"I can taste *this*. What's this one?"

"It's called Wooly Lamb. Chunks of lamb shoulder covered with transparent noodles."

She took a tweezer-bite.

"Mmmm, crispy. And a little creepy. This?"

"Twice-fried flounder."

"Oh, couldn't get it right the first time, eh?"

Round the table she went, tasting every single dish, wanting me to know that not only was she acknowledging these little gifts to her, but that she was accepting them.

"Do you like having all these people here?"

"I *love* having all these people here" she said and
laughed as though it were '57 all over again.
To me she stepped out of the pages of Scott Fitzgerald,
and we were all wearing that gold hat and bouncing
as high as we could to move her. She was an aristocrat
with a blue collar laugh and a stable boy's libido.
The mother I never had, girlfriend I could only dream
about, perfect wife, if only we'd lived in Louisiana—
and she'd wanted it...and that golden hair blowing in
the breeze not only on Kip's sailboat on the Cape but
all those years ago as a nine year old on the beach when
she first captivated me.
Meals can cause trouble, foment argument, rupture
families. But at their best they comfort and unite.

*(He X to fridge, retrieves tomato sorbet tray, X to table D L,
and sets a sorbet at each place setting.)*

I haven't been able to see any of her movies since, and
don't want to, preferring to keep her alive in my mind,
which she is to this day as much as she was before she
gently stopped breathing so many years ago last July
at age fifty-six. But I keep being told by people how
good she is in *Days of Wine and Roses* and another Kazan
movie, *Wild River*, and as Churchill's mother in *Jennie*
and in the droll, dark comedy *Nutcracker* made for T V.
So one of these days I will. And you shouldn't wait for
me.

*(The oven timer goes off, and he retrieves the apple pancake.
Let 'Em In plays. He flips the pancake, tossing it as high as
he can.)*

Can you believe I ate this entire thing that Christmas
day? Maybe you're wondering why this song keeps
cropping up. When the Beatles broke up a hundred
and eighty years ago, it was very sad—our cultural
role models preaching peace and love who wound up
hating each other. Paul immediately started his own

band, and one of his early albums included a song
called *Let 'Em In.*

(He sings along while changing from apron to dinner jacket.)

(Paul McCartney O S)
Someone's knocking at the door
Somebody's ringing in the bell
Someone's knocking at the door
Somebody's ringing the bell
Do me a favour, open the door and let 'em in
Sister Suzie, Brother John
Martin Luther, Phil and Don
Uncle Ernie, Uncle Ian
Open the door and let 'em in
Sister Suzie, Brother John
Martin Luther, Phil and Don
Brother Michael, Auntie Jin
Open the door and let 'em i—n oh yeah...

I was so distraught by the break-up that I invented
deconstructionism on the spot and decided that with
this song he was forgiving everyone and welcoming
them back—John, Ringo, George, even the dreaded
Yoko, together with the man who invented
Protestantism, the Everly brothers, and an old auntie.
And I realize I, too, should let 'em in. I see now this
feast isn't just for Red and Eddie and Frank and Nancy.
You can't exorcise your demons...so you might as well
have 'em in for dinner.

(The doorbell rings. He starts to panic.)

But the real question is—what happens next? I think the
food will be all right, but what if somebody doesn't like
frozen tomatoes or somebody brings up sustainable
farming or the war or whether Fox News is more
reliable 'cause you know where they stand or less?
I mean, what if my mother's passivity puts in an
appearance or my father's ruthlessness or what if my

kids say, "This is what we needed all along, Dad, and never got?"

(The doorbell rings more insistently.)

And what if my divorce comes up or the new love of my life...

(The doorbell rings twice, very insistently. He runs X D S C with turkey on the platter.)

I dunno—

(He lifts the turkey high just as the music builds, and the table slides out, set for many guests)

Life, man!

(Blackout)

(Curtain)

END OF PLAY

www.ingramcontent.com/pod-product-compliance
Lightning Source LLC
Chambersburg PA
CBHW070034110426
42741CB00035B/2768